SAINT OF AVILA DEVOTION NOVENA PRAYER BOOK HER LIFE AND WISDOM

CONTENT

DAY 4: NAVIGATING SPIRITUAL CHALLENGES

. LEARNING FROM ST. TERESA'S EXPERIENCES WITH SPIRITUAL TRIALS

. PRAYER FOR STRENGTH AND PERSEVERANCE IN TIMES OF DIFFICULTY

DAY 5: SURRENDERING TO GOD'S WILL

. STUDYING ST. TERESA'S TEACHINGS ON SURRENDERING TO GOD'S PLAN

. PRAYER FOR TRUST AND SURRENDER TO GOD'S DIVINE WILL

DAY 6: GROWING IN LOVE AND COMPASSION

. REFLECTING ON ST. TERESA'S EMPHASIS ON LOVE AND COMPASSION

. PRAYER FOR AN OPEN HEART TO LOVE AND SERVE OTHERS

DAY 7: FOSTERING INNER TRANSFORMATION

. EXPLORING ST. TERESA'S THOUGHTS ON SPIRITUAL GROWTH AND TRANSFORMATION

. PRAYER FOR PERSONAL GROWTH AND RENEWAL IN CHRIST

DAY 8: ENCOUNTERING GOD'S PRESENCE

. MEDITATING ON ST. TERESA'S EXPERIENCES
OF ENCOUNTERING GOD'S PRESENCE

. PRAYER FOR A PROFOUND ENCOUNTER WITH
GOD IN OUR LIVES

DAY 9: EMBRACING THE INTERIOR CASTLE

. REFLECTING ON ST. TERESA'S SPIRITUAL
JOURNEY THROUGH THE "INTERIOR CASTLE"

. PRAYER FOR THE GRACE TO ENTER AND
EXPLORE OUR OWN INTERIOR CASTLE

. CONCLUSION

INTRODUCTION

Welcome to this nine-day novena dedicated to St. Teresa of Avila, a remarkable mystic, writer, and saint of the Catholic Church. Throughout her life, St. Teresa exemplified a profound love for God and an unwavering commitment to deepening her spiritual journey. Her insights, writings, and experiences continue to inspire countless individuals seeking a closer relationship with the Divine.

During this novena, we will embark on a journey of reflection, prayer, and contemplation, delving into the teachings and wisdom of St. Teresa. Each day, we will explore different aspects of her spirituality, gaining insight into her profound understanding of prayer, humility, love, and transformation. As we follow in her footsteps, may we be drawn closer to God and find guidance for our own spiritual path.

St. Teresa of Avila invites us to journey inward, to explore the depths of our souls, and to encounter the presence of God within the chambers of our hearts. Through her writings, she guides us in embracing the challenges and joys of our spiritual pilgrimage, reminding us that the journey itself is a sacred and transformative experience.

Let us begin this novena with open hearts and minds, ready to receive the grace and inspiration that St. Teresa offers. May her life story and teachings inspire us to seek a more profound union with God and to live lives filled with love, compassion, and purpose. As we embark on this novena, may we find solace, guidance, and encouragement on our own path of faith.

Let us begin our novena, invoking the intercession of St. Teresa of Avila, as we seek to draw closer to God and to embrace the transformative journey that lies ahead.

OVERVIEW OF ST. TERESA OF AVILA AND HER SIGNIFICANCE

St. Teresa of Avila (1515–1582) was a Spanish mystic, writer, and reformer, best known for her profound spiritual insights, writings, and contributions to Catholic theology. She was born in Gotarrendura, Spain, and entered the Carmelite Order at a young age. St. Teresa's spiritual journey led her to seek a more contemplative and intimate relationship with God.

She experienced a series of powerful mystical encounters and visions, which she documented in her autobiographical works, most notably in "The Life of Teresa of Jesus." St. Teresa's writings emphasize the importance of inner prayer, humility, and the pursuit of divine union.

In response to the challenges she observed within the Church, St. Teresa initiated a reform movement within the Carmelite Order. She founded the Discalced Carmelites (Barefoot Carmelites), which sought to return to the order's original contemplative and austere ideals.

St. Teresa's literary legacy includes works like "The Interior Castle," where she presents a metaphorical exploration of the stages of spiritual growth and union with God. Her writings have had a profound influence on Christian spirituality, inspiring countless individuals to deepen their prayer life and seek a more intimate connection with God.

St. Teresa of Avila was canonized in 1614 and later declared a Doctor of the Church in 1970, recognizing her significant contributions to Christian theology and her enduring impact on the spiritual lives of believers. Her feast day is 15th October.

HOW TO PRAY THE NOVENA

Praying a novena to St. Teresa of Avila involves dedicating nine consecutive days to reflection, prayer, and contemplation, focusing on specific themes related to her life and spirituality. Here's a general guide on how to pray the novena:

Preparation: Choose a quiet and comfortable place where you can spend a few moments in reflection and prayer each day for the duration of the novena.

Novena Intentions: Decide on your specific intentions for the novena. These could be personal requests, spiritual growth, guidance, or any other matters you wish to bring before St. Teresa and God.

Day-by-Day Guide:

Read: Begin each day by reading the designated reflection for that day from your chosen novena source or table of contents.

Reflect: Spend a few moments contemplating the message of the day's reflection. Consider how it applies to your own life and spiritual journey.

Pray: Offer a heartfelt prayer based on the theme of the day's reflection. You can use a pre-written prayer, compose your own, or speak directly to God and St. Teresa.

Personal Reflection: After the prayer, take some time to quietly reflect on the words you've read and the prayer you've offered. Consider how you can apply the insights from St. Teresa to your life.

Repeat: Continue this process for each of the nine days, focusing on the specific themes outlined in the novena.

Closing Prayer: On the final day of the novena, spend some extra time in reflection and prayer, thanking God and St. Teresa for their guidance and intercession. You can also ask for continued help in applying the insights you've gained.

Follow-Up: After completing the novena, remain open to the ongoing inspiration and guidance you've received. Consider incorporating St. Teresa's teachings into your daily life and continuing to deepen your relationship with God.

Remember that while there are traditional prayers associated with the novena, you can also personalize your prayers and reflections based on your own thoughts and feelings. The novena is a flexible and meaningful way to connect with St. Teresa of Avila's spirituality and seek her intercession in your life.

EACH DAY OF
YOUR
NOVENA
PRAYERS
BEGIN WITH
SIGN OF
CROSS

NOVENA PRAYERS

DAY 1

SEEKING DIVINE GUIDANCE

Reflection: Today, we begin our novena by contemplating the importance of seeking divine guidance in our lives. St. Teresa of Avila's journey was marked by her unwavering quest to draw closer to God and discern His will. She encourages us to turn to God with open hearts, seeking His guidance in all aspects of our existence.

In our fast-paced world, it's easy to become entangled in the noise and distractions around us. St. Teresa reminds us that true wisdom comes from seeking the Divine, and that our connection with God can serve as a compass through life's challenges.

Prayer: Heavenly Father, as we embark on this novena, we humbly ask for your guidance and wisdom. Like St. Teresa, help us to seek your presence in all things and to discern your will for our lives. Grant us the grace to be still and listen to your gentle voice amid the chaos of the world. St. Teresa of Avila, intercede for us and guide us in our journey towards deeper communion with God. Amen.

Take a few moments to reflect on the guidance you are seeking from God. Offer your intentions and listen to His response in the silence of your heart.

DAY 2
EMBRACING HUMILITY

Reflection: Today, we reflect on the virtue of humility, a quality St. Teresa of Avila held dear. She understood that true spiritual progress is rooted in a humble heart, one that acknowledges its limitations and places complete trust in God. St. Teresa teaches us that humility opens the door to divine grace and enables us to draw closer to the Creator.

In a world that often values self-promotion and pride, St. Teresa's example challenges us to cultivate an attitude of humility, recognizing that all our gifts and talents are ultimately bestowed upon us by God.

Prayer: Gracious God, we come before you with humble hearts, recognizing our need for your guidance and grace. Teach us, like St. Teresa, to embrace humility as a pathway to true greatness. Help us to let go of our ego and pride, and to place our complete trust in your divine providence. St. Teresa of Avila, pray for us, that we may learn to walk humbly in your footsteps and in the light of God's love. Amen.

Take a few moments to reflect on the areas of your life where humility is needed. Ask for the strength to embrace humility and to trust in God's plan for you.

DAY 3
DEEPENING INNER PRAYER

Reflection: Today, we delve into the practice of inner prayer, a central aspect of St. Teresa of Avila's spirituality. She believed that through cultivating a deep and intimate connection with God in the silence of our hearts, we can experience profound union with the Divine. St. Teresa's writings reveal her insights into the transformative power of inner prayer, where our souls become a dwelling place for God's presence.

As we reflect on inner prayer, let us remember that it is not about elaborate words or rituals, but rather about opening ourselves to a personal and intimate encounter with God.

Prayer: Loving God, you invite us into the depths of our hearts to commune with you in quietude and stillness. Grant us the grace, like St. Teresa, to deepen our inner prayer, allowing your presence to fill us completely. May our innermost thoughts and desires be offered to you in this sacred space of communion. St. Teresa of Avila, guide us in the art of inner prayer, that we may draw ever closer to your divine love. Amen.

Take a few moments to engage in inner prayer. Set aside distractions, quiet your mind, and open your heart to God's presence. Allow your innermost thoughts and feelings to be offered to Him in this intimate encounter.

DAY 4

NAVIGATING SPIRITUAL CHALLENGES

Reflection: In our journey of faith, we encounter various spiritual challenges that can test our resolve and deepen our trust in God. St. Teresa of Avila faced her own trials and tribulations, which she embraced as opportunities for growth. She teaches us that challenges, though difficult, can lead us to a closer relationship with God, as they draw us into greater reliance on His strength.

Today, as we reflect on navigating spiritual challenges, let us remember that even in times of difficulty, God's grace is present to sustain and guide us.

Prayer: Heavenly Father, when we face spiritual challenges, grant us the courage and perseverance to continue seeking you. Just as St. Teresa overcame obstacles on her path, may we turn to you in times of trial and find strength in your unwavering love. Help us to trust that every challenge is an opportunity to draw nearer to you. St. Teresa of Avila, intercede for us, that we may navigate life's challenges with faith and resilience. Amen.

Take a few moments to reflect on the spiritual challenges you have faced or are currently facing. Offer them to God in prayer, asking for His guidance and strength to overcome them.

DAY 5
SURRENDERING TO GOD'S WILL

Reflection: Surrendering to God's will is a fundamental aspect of St. Teresa of Avila's spirituality. She understood that true freedom and peace come when we align our desires with God's plan for us. St. Teresa's life exemplified a profound trust in God's providence, even in the face of uncertainty.

Today, let us reflect on the importance of surrendering our will to God, allowing His divine wisdom to guide our lives.

Prayer: Gracious Lord, help us to relinquish our own desires and plans, and to embrace your will with open hearts. Just as St. Teresa found freedom in surrender, may we too experience the peace that comes from entrusting our lives to your loving care. Grant us the grace to let go and allow your divine purpose to unfold. St. Teresa of Avila, pray for us, that we may surrender our lives completely to God's loving embrace. Amen.

Take a few moments to consider areas in your life where you struggle to surrender to God's will. Pray for the grace to trust His plan and to find peace in aligning your desires with His purpose.

DAY 6

GROWING IN LOVE AND COMPASSION

Reflection: Love and compassion were at the heart of St. Teresa of Avila's teachings. She emphasized the importance of cultivating a genuine love for God and for our fellow human beings. St. Teresa's life demonstrated that love and compassion are powerful forces that can transform hearts and bring healing to the world.

Today, let us reflect on how we can grow in love and compassion, following St. Teresa's example of selfless care for others.

Prayer: Loving Father, you call us to love one another as you have loved us. Grant us the grace, like St. Teresa, to grow in love and compassion for those around us. May our hearts be open to the needs of others, and may our actions reflect the selfless love that you have shown us. St. Teresa of Avila, inspire us to be instruments of your compassion in the world. Amen.

Take a few moments to think about how you can demonstrate love and compassion to those in your life. Pray for the grace to embody these virtues and make a positive impact on the lives of others.

DAY 7

FOSTERING INNER TRANSFORMATION

Reflection: St. Teresa of Avila believed in the transformative power of a life dedicated to God. She described the soul as a "mansion" with many rooms, symbolizing the different stages of spiritual growth. St. Teresa encourages us to actively cooperate with God's grace, allowing Him to transform us from within.

Today, let us reflect on how we can foster inner transformation and cooperate with God's work in our lives.

Prayer: Heavenly Father, you are the master of our souls and the source of our transformation. As we journey through the various rooms of our inner mansion, may we embrace the changes you bring about with trust and openness. Just as St. Teresa underwent inner transformation, help us to surrender to your loving guidance and become more fully conformed to your image. St. Teresa of Avila, pray for us, that we may allow God's transformative power to work within us. Amen.

Take a few moments to consider areas in your life where you desire inner transformation. Pray for the grace to cooperate with God's work and to be open to the changes He wants to bring about in your heart and soul.

DAY 8

ENCOUNTERING GOD'S PRESENCE

Reflection: St. Teresa of Avila's life was marked by her profound encounters with the presence of God. She believed that through prayer and contemplation, we can experience a deep communion with the Divine. St. Teresa's writings invite us to seek moments of intimacy with God, where we can feel His loving presence surrounding us.

Today, let us reflect on the beauty of encountering God's presence and the transformative impact it can have on our lives.

Prayer: Gracious God, you are present in every aspect of our lives, waiting to reveal your love to us. As we reflect on St. Teresa's encounters with your presence, may we too yearn for those moments of communion with you. Grant us the grace to open our hearts to your presence and to recognize your love in the quiet moments of our lives. St. Teresa of Avila, intercede for us, that we may encounter your presence and experience the joy of your love. Amen.

Take a few moments to enter into a quiet and contemplative space. Open your heart to God's presence and invite Him to reveal Himself to you in this moment of prayer. Allow yourself to be receptive to His love and grace.

DAY 9

EMBRACING THE INTERIOR CASTLE

Reflection: In her famous work "The Interior Castle," St. Teresa of Avila presents a metaphorical journey of the soul towards union with God. Each chamber within the castle represents a stage of spiritual growth and a deeper level of intimacy with the Divine. St. Teresa invites us to explore the innermost chambers of our hearts, where God's presence resides.

As we conclude this novena, let us reflect on the concept of the Interior Castle and how we can continue to deepen our relationship with God.

Prayer: Heavenly Father, you have invited us to embark on a journey within ourselves, where we can encounter your presence and draw closer to you. As we contemplate the symbolism of the Interior Castle, may we be inspired to explore the depths of our hearts and to seek union with you. Just as St. Teresa envisioned the chambers of the castle, guide us in our ongoing quest for spiritual growth and intimacy with you. St. Teresa of Avila, pray for us, that we may fully embrace the journey within and discover the treasures of your love. Amen.

Take a few moments to meditate on the concept of the Interior Castle and the stages of spiritual growth it represents. Reflect on how you can continue to deepen your relationship with God and explore the inner chambers of your heart in the days and weeks ahead.

CONCLUSION

As we conclude this novena dedicated to St. Teresa of Avila, let us take a moment to reflect on the insights we've gained and the journey we've embarked upon. Throughout these nine days, we have explored themes of seeking divine guidance, embracing humility, deepening inner prayer, navigating spiritual challenges, surrendering to God's will, growing in love and compassion, fostering inner transformation, encountering God's presence, and embracing the concept of the Interior Castle.

St. Teresa of Avila's life and teachings have inspired us to draw closer to God, to cultivate humility, and to open our hearts to the transformative power of His love. Her wisdom reminds us that the path of spirituality is a journey of continual growth and exploration, marked by moments of encounter, challenge, and surrender.

As we move forward, may we carry the lessons of this novena with us, applying them to our daily lives and seeking to deepen our connection with God. Let us continue to embrace the journey within, exploring the chambers of our own hearts as we seek to encounter the presence of the Divine.

May the intercession of St. Teresa of Avila guide us on our spiritual path, and may her example inspire us to live lives of greater love, compassion, and inner transformation. Let us go forth with renewed hope and determination, trusting in God's guidance and grace.

We offer this conclusion in gratitude for the opportunity to reflect, pray, and grow in the company of St. Teresa of Avila. May her legacy continue to inspire us in the days ahead. Amen.

Made in the USA
Las Vegas, NV
18 November 2024

12039711R10017